Planet Earth

Earth Fact File

Earth is 4.5 billion years old

71% is covered by water

It is the only planet in
the solar system that has life

Written by Dan Green

Illustrated by Sean Sims

EGMONT

We bring stories to life

Book Band: Gold

Adapted from *The Adventures of Earth* first published in Great Britain 2016

Planet Earth first published in Great Britain 2017
by Red Shed, an imprint of Egmont UK Limited
The Yellow Building, 1 Nicholas Road, London W11 4AN

www.egmont.co.uk

ISBN 978 1 4052 8495 0

A CIP catalogue record for this book is available from The British Library.

Printed in Singapore
65794/1

Series and book banding consultant: Nikki Gamble

 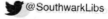

Planet
Earth

Contents

Introduction

Earth has been around for a very, very long time. About 4.5 billion years ago, it formed along with the other planets in the solar system that travel around the Sun. Like you, this rocky planet has changed a lot since its early years.

Earth begins

Earth formed from a huge cloud of dust and gas spinning around a brand new star – the young Sun. Gravity caused the dust and debris to clump together into the planets in our solar system.

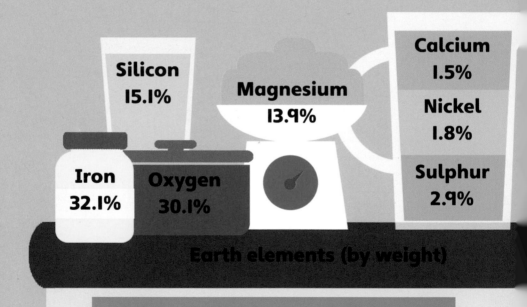

Silicon
15.1%

Magnesium
13.9%

Calcium
1.5%

Nickel
1.8%

Iron
32.1%

Oxygen
30.1%

Sulphur
2.9%

Earth elements (by weight)

RECIPE FOR PLANET EARTH
3 parts iron
3 parts oxygen
1.5 parts silicon
an equal amount of magnesium
a sprinkling of other elements

Trace
amounts
of other
elements
1.2%

luminium
1.4%

Mix dry elements, heat vigorously and
allow to settle for 100 million years.
Cool slowly and watch as the surface
slowly becomes wet with water.

Asteroid smash

Earth's many collisions with space rocks in its early years stopped life developing. However, they may have brought water to the planet.

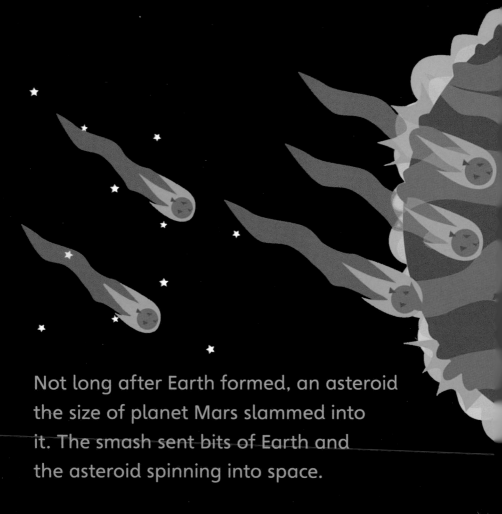

Not long after Earth formed, an asteroid the size of planet Mars slammed into it. The smash sent bits of Earth and the asteroid spinning into space.

The gas, dust and rock chunks from the smash drew together to become our Moon. The Moon travels round Earth in a circle called an orbit.

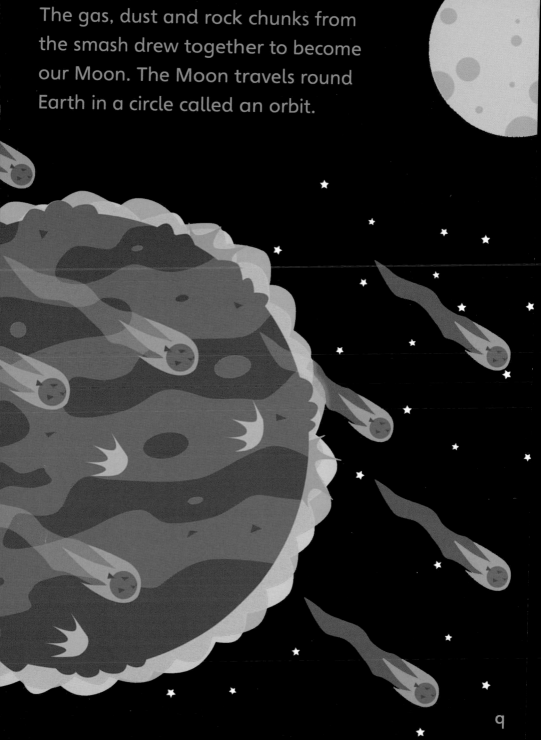

A goldilocks planet

Earth's many collisions with space rocks may have brought water to the planet. As Earth cooled, clouds formed and rain began to shape Earth's crust. Life began in the oceans and bacteria started to fill the atmosphere with oxygen.

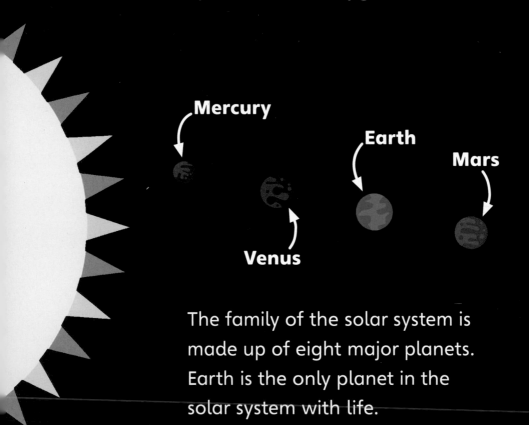

Mercury

Earth

Mars

Venus

The family of the solar system is made up of eight major planets. Earth is the only planet in the solar system with life.

Temperatures are warm enough to melt ice, but cool enough not to boil all the water away. Astronomers call this 'not-too-hot-not-too-cold' region of space the Goldilocks zone.

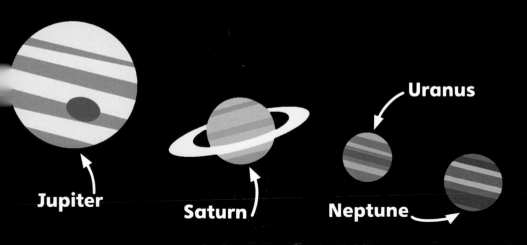

Blue planet

Earth is squashed and bulges out in the middle – a bit like an orange. Today, oceans cover almost three-quarters (71 per cent) of the planet's surface. Because of this water, Earth is known as the Blue Planet.

Equator

Time for light from the Sun to reach Earth:
8 minutes, 18 seconds

Size around the middle:

40.075km

Day length:
23 hours,
56 minutes,
4.1 seconds

Year length:
365.25 days

Earth in a day

Imagine the whole of Earth's history squeezed into a day. The planet is born as the clock strikes midnight, 4.5 billion years ago. Humans don't show up until 11.59pm the following night.

Scientists think life must have started in a sheltered spot where chemicals could react to produce living things. This may have been where hydrothermal 'smokers' on the ocean floor pump out life-giving, nutrient-rich seawater

3.8 billion year ago
The current 'best guess'
for the start of life on Earth

Bacteria

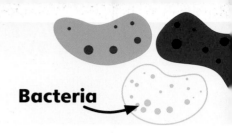

3.5 billion year ago
First plants appear

535 million years ago
Big burst of ocean life

252-66 million years ago
Age of the dinosaurs

220 million years ago
First mammals appear

2.8 million years ago
First humans walk on Earth

Life on Earth

Every part of the planet, from the icy
poles to the steamy tropics, has some
form of life living on it. The zone of
life on Earth is called the biosphere.
It extends from high in the atmosphere
to deep underground.

All living things face a fight to survive. They
must find food, avoid danger and make babies.
Some species, such as the Tasmanian tiger,
have become extinct. Farmers killed it because
they thought it was a danger to their sheep.

The highest flying bird is the Rüppell's griffon vulture, from Africa. It can soar up to 11.3km high in the sky.

The devil worm is one of the deepest living animals on land. One was found 3.6km underground, in a South African gold mine.

Earth is built like an onion. The outer shell, or crust, is a thin layer of hard rock. The rocks of the mantle underneath form the thickest layer. The outer core is a shell of hot, liquid metal that surrounds the solid inner core.

Crust (up to 50km thick)

Mantle (2,900km thick)

Outer core (2,300km thick)

Inner core (1,200km thick)

Crushing pressure keeps the iron and nickel core solid despite the high temperatures.

Inside the planet

Things may look calm on the surface, but Earth is full of energy. The temperature at the centre of the planet may be as much as 6,000°C. Over millions of years, the effects can be dramatic.

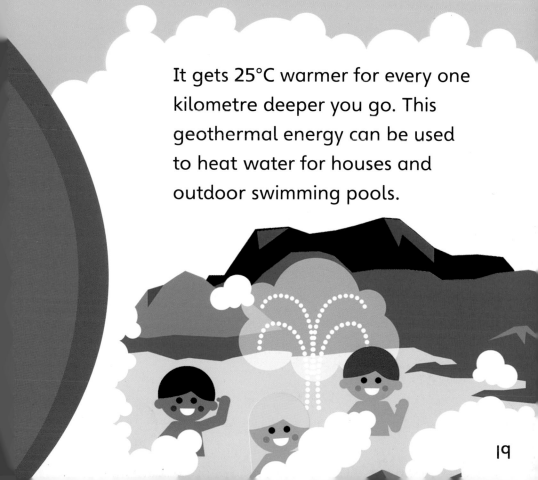

It gets 25°C warmer for every one kilometre deeper you go. This geothermal energy can be used to heat water for houses and outdoor swimming pools.

Volcanoes

Most of the action on Earth happens where tectonic plates meet. Volcanoes mostly occur at places where tectonic plates pull apart or bump together.

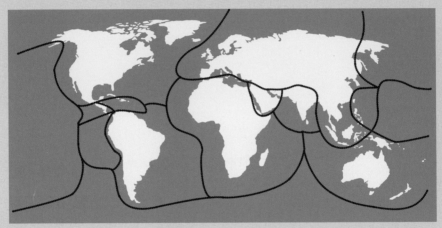

Tectonic plates floating on the surface of the planet are in constant motion, driven by the heat from inside the Earth. There are 8 major plates and many smaller ones.

One in 10 people in the world live in the 'danger range' of an active volcano.

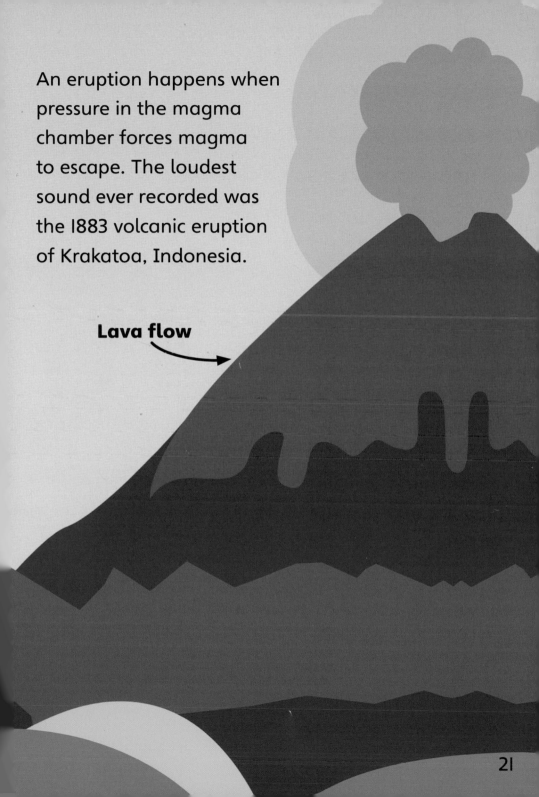

An eruption happens when pressure in the magma chamber forces magma to escape. The loudest sound ever recorded was the 1883 volcanic eruption of Krakatoa, Indonesia.

Lava flow

Earthquakes

Earthquakes happen when forces in the crust move great masses of rock. Pressure builds up that, when released, sends out shockwaves of energy that shake the surface of the planet.

Most earthquake activity happens at the boundaries between tectonic plates. The strength of earthquakes is measured on the Richter Scale.

All at sea

Almost three-quarters of the planet's surface is covered in water. This marine habitat, or biome, is the largest on the planet. The oceans are vital to the way the Earth works and for our survival too.

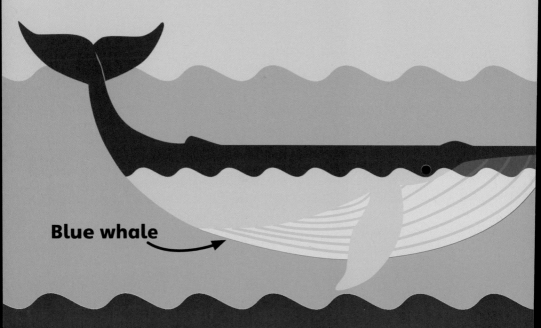

Blue whale

There are five main oceans: the Arctic, Atlantic, Indian, Pacific and Southern, as well as lots of smaller seas. Each one has different zones at different depths.

Sunlight zone
Surface to 200m
This zone receives lots of sunlight, so over 90 percent of ocean life lives here.

Twilight zone
200m to 1,000m
Not much life lives here because only a tiny amount of light reaches the zone.

Midnight zone
1,000m and deeper
It is pitch-black here, the only glow coming from squid, jellyfish and microbes.

Weather and climate

Around half a million observations of the atmosphere are needed every day to predict the weather. These come from weather stations all around the world and satellites in orbit.

High pressure
Cool air sinks, pressing down on the surface. High-pressure areas tend to bring dry and settled weather.

Low pressure
Warm air rises. Rising air presses down less, making low-pressure areas. This often brings stormy, rainy weather with it.

Climate is the average weather in a particular area. A region's climate depends on its average temperatures, pressures and precipitation (rainfall, snowfall etc).

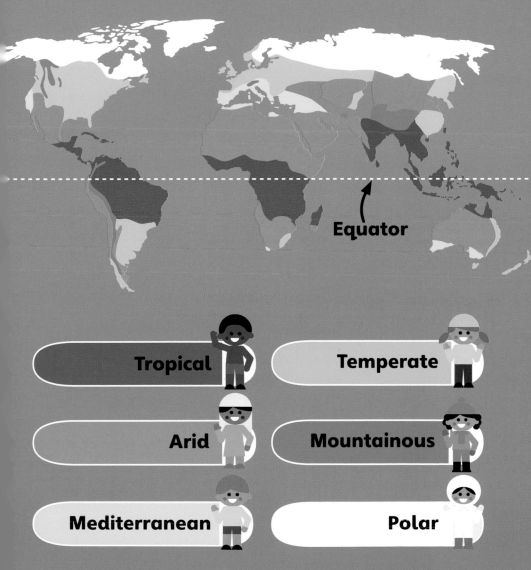

Equator

Tropical

Temperate

Arid

Mountainous

Mediterranean

Polar

Looking after Earth

There are things that all of us can do around the house to look after our planet and conserve natural resources.

Water butt

Save water by taking a short shower instead of a bath. Use a water butt to collect rainwater. Save energy by turning off lights and using low energy lightbulbs.

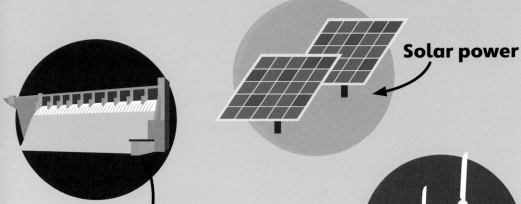

Solar power

Hydroelectric power

Wind power

Some forms of energy will never run out, unlike the fossil fuels – coal, oil and gas. By using wind, solar and water power, we are looking after the planet.

Bins for recycling

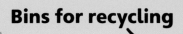

Recycle or reuse as many things as possible – a plastic bag takes 10–20 years to decompose.

29

Glossary

astronomer   A scientist who studies the universe and the objects in it.

atmosphere   The mixture of gases that surrounds Earth.

asteroid   A rocky body that moves around the Sun.

bacteria   One-celled organisms found everywhere on Earth.

biome   A large community of plants and animals that occupy a particular area.

biosphere   The part of Earth's crust, waters and atmosphere that supports life.

debris   Fragments or rubble of something that has broken up.

Fun facts

Earth's toughest animal is the tardigrade. It can survive at below −200°C or up to 151°C, as well as in space!

element   A substance that cannot be separated into simpler substances by chemical means.

eruption   The release of gas, ash and lava onto the surface from a volcano.

extinct   No longer in existence.

hydrothermal   Describes water heated underground by Earth's internal heat.

magma   Hot, melted rock, usually formed in Earth's upper mantle.

nutrient   A substance that is needed for growth and a healthy life.

solar system   Our Sun, together with all the planets and other bodies that revolve around it.

star   An object in the night sky that sends out its own light.

Our Moon is drifting away from Earth at about 4cm per year. That's about four times slower than your hair grows.

Index